Kieran the Pirate

by Cleo deLancey

Copyright © 2014 by Cleo deLancey

First Edition – 2014

ISBN

978-1-4602-1243-1 (Paperback)

978-1-4602-1244-8 (eBook)

All rights reserved.

No part of this publication may be reproduced in any form, or by any means, electronic or mechanical, including photocopying, recording, or any information browsing, storage, or retrieval system, without permission in writing from the publisher.

Produced by:

FriesenPress

Suite 300 – 852 Fort Street

Victoria, BC, Canada V8W 1H8

www.friesenpress.com

Distributed to the trade by The Ingram Book Company

Kieran the Pirate

by Cleo deLancey

Especially for Kieran

and

To the Stewart and deLancey families

"I want to be a scary pirate," said Kieran,

"but all I could find is this cool pirate hat.

I hope I can scare someone!"

"Arrr!

Did I scare you?"

Kieran asked his brother Seth.

"No," replied Seth, "You're not a very scary pirate. You need an earring."

"Arrr!

Did I scare you?"

Kieran asked his aunty Erin.

"No," said his aunty.
"You're not a very scary pirate.
You need a pirate shirt."

"Arrrr!

Did I scare you?"

Kieran asked his grandfther Tom.

"No," said Grandpa.

"You're not a very scary pirate.

You need an eye patch."

"ARrrr!

did I scare you?"

Kieran asked his grandmother Bonnie.

"No dear," replied Grandma, "You're not a very scary pirate. You need a sash."

"ARRrr!

Did I scare you?"

Kieran asked his uncle Adam.

"No," said Adam, "You're not a very scary pirate. You need a cutlass!"

"ARRR!

Did I scare you?"

Kieran asked his great-grandfather Cliff.

"No lad," said Great-Grandpa, "You're not a very scary pirate. You need some pirate boots!"

"ARRR!

Did I scare you?"

Kieran asked his mother Tara.

"No son," she replied, "You're not a very scary pirate. You need a parrot."

"ARRR!!

Did I scare you?"

Kieran asked his baby cousin Nigel.

BUT the baby just cried!

"At last," shouted Kieran.

"I am a **very** **scary** **PIRATE!**"

Lightning Source UK Ltd.
Milton Keynes UK
UKIC01n0200110615
253228UK00002B/8